Yesterday I was Pregnant: What I Wish I'd Known About Miscarriage Before it Happened to Me.

Vanessa Bailey

Published by Vanessa Bailey, 2017.

Dedication

D edicated to mommies everywhere who know the pain of loss; together we are stronger.

Psalm 56:8
You keep track of all my sorrows.
You have collected all my tears in your bottle.
You have recorded each one in your book.

Chapter One: You're Not Alone

Whether you've had one or numerous miscarriages, are afraid you may have one, are in the process of having one, are a partner to someone who had a miscarriage, have a friend who experienced a miscarriage, or are just curious about what people who experience miscarriage have gone through – this book is for you. Miscarriage took me by surprise when I least expected it, and there are so many things that I wish somebody had told me before it happened. There were opportunities, both via healthcare professionals and also personal acquaintances, that somebody could have filled me in or given me the scoop on what a miscarriage entails. But nobody did.

I have never felt so alone or inexplicably numb as I did when I had a miscarriage. There is so much that your body experiences, both physically and emotionally; some of it rather quickly, and some all too slowly. As though the physical experience of enduring a miscarriage is not enough, there's the emotional that comes with it free of charge. The emotional aspect of miscarriage is the ugly "free gift" that you sometimes find at the bottom of your bag when you've been shopping somewhere. The item nobody wanted to buy, so they slip it in the bottom of the bag without giving you a chance to "No thanks," and you end up with it at home; wondering why you even have it in the first place. And then, if you have a partner or significant other who is experiencing the miscarriage with you, it adds a whole new twist that you must take hold of and deal with as well.

For whatever reason, miscarriage is one of those cultural taboos that our society has somehow interpreted to not be appropriate dinner conversation. There are many topics of conversation that are this way; realities of life that we just handle on our own because it doesn't seem like something to "bring up" and chat with other people about. Our society has for whatever reason molded these taboos to be things we naturally know not to bring up, and causes us to feel ashamed to some degree if they happen to us. I'm here to tell you that this is the opposite of what needs to happen when it comes to miscarriage. Miscarriage needs people, laughs, friendly faces, familiar hugs, and reassurance when nothing in life seems bearable.

If you're reading this book, it likely means that miscarriage has touched you in some way, no matter what that way may be. Miscarriage needs to be okay to talk about. It is not something to be ashamed of. It is not something you did wrong. It is not even something you could have prevented. In fact, it's actually quite natural and quite normal; one of the ways the human body finds its way of selectively choosing whether to continue investment in something that may be damaged in some way.

You will need help. Your partner or significant other will need help. It's okay. I promise. You are not alone, and you don't need to feel like you are. I looked for books that I could read to help me when I was going through my miscarriage, and nothing seemed to fit the bill to help with what I was looking for. My hope and prayer is that this book helps you, even if it is only in some small way. I want you to know that you are normal, what you've been through is normal, what you're feeling is normal... and mostly that despite all those "normals," there is nothing about miscarriage that feels or is actually normal at all. It's simply not the way things are supposed to be. Yet, somehow it still is.

You will feel just about every known emotion throughout the process; guilt, shame, dread, fear, sorrow, gut wrenching despair, hopelessness, sadness, relief, pain, etc. And they're all normal things to feel. Hang in there. Read on. It's going to be okay. You will make it. And hopefully after you've read this book, you'll feel better. Some sense of relief. If only for a moment. Most importantly; you'll know. You'll know what I wished I had known before and during my miscarriage. And you can share what you learned with somebody else and hopefully help them as well. We have to stick together when it comes to miscarriage. It may knock us down for a moment, but we can get up and fight back by taking control of our lives again and pressing onward.

Here's to you and the journey you are facing. I'm with you.

Chapter Two: To Beat or Not to Beat

After two previous successful pregnancies resulting in three beautiful babies, I had taken my third pregnancy for granted right from the beginning. My first pregnancy was the result of a honeymoon production, and consisted of 40 uneventful weeks and a beautiful baby boy. My second pregnancy, somewhat more complicated, was the result of a gestational surrogacy. I had no trouble getting pregnant that time either (the assistance of science and medical professionals made sure of that), and successfully carried two healthy and handsome boys for 38 weeks until I delivered and then passed them off to their wonderful, loving, hope filled parents. Though that pregnancy was difficult purely given the fact that I was carrying twins and the normal tolls that takes on a woman's body, it was rather uneventful as well and there was nothing unusual to report or be concerned about. My third pregnancy came when my husband and I determined we were ready to add another baby to our family. As expected, we didn't have any trouble conceiving and before we knew it were making the announcement that we were eight weeks pregnant; sharing the exciting news with our closest family and friends.

In my first two pregnancies, I had experienced morning sickness for about 12 weeks. I am one of the lucky ones – ha! It's not really morning sickness at all. I like to call it "worse in the morning sickness" because in reality, it's all the time. The only difference is, in the morning I may actually be sick and end up visiting the nearest bathroom or trash can (whatever is closer). It came on about 6 weeks into the pregnancy, almost to the day both times, and lasted well into the second trimester before dwindling off and only occasionally bothering me. With the twins, my nausea was twice as bad and I actually had to take prescribed anti-nausea medication in order to be able to successfully eat and gain weight.

This pregnancy, when 6 weeks came and went with no morning sickness to report, the lingering question of whether everything was okay was beginning to weigh in the back of my mind. I had all of the other normal pregnancy symptoms in tow, and there were no concerns to note to date, so for the most part I didn't think anything of it and just carried on as usual. I mentioned my concern to only a few people, who brushed it off as "Maybe it's finally a girl!" and we carried on as usual. Each time I began to feel a little worry start seeping into my thoughts, I reminded myself of just how many times I'd heard that girl vs. boy pregnancies were different; one often resulting in morning sickness while the other didn't for the same woman.

At my ten-week routine doctor's appointment for the pregnancy, which in this case happened to be the one that consisted of a physical examination, the provider made the determination that everything was going well to date and there were no concerns to report, as I expected. Body looked good, history was good, bloodwork looked fine, urine test revealed nothing; everything was in order. The final event for the appointment was to hear the heartbeat for the first time! She got out the Doppler fetal heart rate monitor to listen for baby's heartbeat. After putting the warm gel on my belly and trying for a few minutes, she found a heartbeat! Quickly followed by a "Whoop. That's yours. Not baby's." Before giving up less than a minute later, she told me not to worry about it. She reassured me that often the baby is still too little to hear the heartbeat at ten weeks old, and usually at 12 weeks there is more of a guarantee that you'll be able to hear it.

My heart sank. In both of my other pregnancies, I'd heard heartbeats prior to 10 weeks. At this point, I mentioned the fact that I'd been somewhat concerned about the lack of morning sickness as this was so characteristic in my other two pregnancies and seemed strangely unusual for me. She took a brief glance at my history and then stated, "Maybe this time it's your girl!" I smiled, as she wasn't even close to the first person who had said that. Seeing as how I'd delivered three boys thus far (two of which weren't even biologically mine), the running joke was that my uterus was only capable of producing boys. But inside, I worried. My mommy heart knew that something wasn't right.

The following week, at 11 weeks and 6 days pregnant, I found myself in the middle of the grocery store trying not to panic. I had been grocery shopping and was nearing the end of an hour-long trip moseying about the store with a cart filled with enough groceries to feed a small army, when I began bleeding. I literally stopped dead in my tracks, numb and paralyzed by disbelief that this was actually happening, as I felt what only women can so easily identify as an unexpected flow. I wanted to tell myself that everything was okay and this was normal. "It happens all the time, to many women, throughout various stages of pregnancy. It happened to me with the twins, and they are fantastic. They are healthy, happy, and now 14 months old. I'm fine. It will be fine."

I rushed to the bathroom, leaving my cart filled with groceries right outside the door and thinking "Great. Just what I needed. A cart filled with groceries, much of it frozen, and now this disaster. I'm going to make a scene regardless of how I get out of here and what that entails." To my dismay, I had already bled through my panties and some on to my shorts. In the excitement of pregnancy, one of the first things I (and I'm sure many other women as well) did was to rid my purse of all pads and tampons. Sort of like a mini early pregnancy celebration. "Screw you guys. Won't be needing you for a while. I'm gonna have a baby! Ha!" At that exact moment in the grocery store bathroom, blood on my hands and pants, I greatly regretted that decision.

I did the best I could with what I had in my purse to hopefully keep things from getting worse between that moment and when I could safely get to the car. I determined that there was not enough blood on my pants to be highly visible, so I could hopefully make it through the check-out (so long as I remembered not to bend over) without being noticed, and then get to the car. I decided to call my husband while I was waiting in line, to let him know what was going on. I didn't really know what was going on, honestly, but I knew I had to embrace the reality somehow, and so I called to give him a heads up. Needless to say, he was as thrilled as I was and silently did his best to do what I knew was his best effort to not panic as well, mostly in hopes of keeping me calm.

Chapter Three: Not Meant to Beat

As I walked toward the emergency room about an hour later, calmly processing my thoughts and trying not to let my mind race, my heart began beating faster and faster. It became less and less possible to control my racing mind and keep myself from being mentally paralyzed; numb after succumbing to all the fears that were fast tracking through my thoughts all at once in a flurry. Everything in me wanted to turn around. "Go back to the car and go home. If I go home, pretend everything is normal, get in bed with my husband and go to sleep; when I wake up tomorrow everything will be fine. This will all just go away. It can't really be happening." I had kept myself relatively calm over the last hour as I prepared to go to the emergency room, but as I walked through the glass double doors, I felt myself start to disintegrate. I knew if I said it out loud, somebody else would know, and the weight of it would hit me like a ton of bricks and suddenly be real. I stopped at the triage desk and took a couple of deep breaths, as the nurse eyed me and waited for an indication of why I was visiting, and then forced the words out. "I'm 12 weeks pregnant. And I'm bleeding." There. I said it. It's out now. It's real. We must handle this. I'm here and they're going to tell me what is going on, whether I want to know or not.

They got me in rather quickly, which is saying something for an emergency room. They drew blood, took a urine sample, and shortly thereafter called me back for an ultrasound. They came to get me in a wheelchair, and then forced me to sit in it. Little by little, they were

9

crumbling the picture of perfection that I had in my mind. There is nothing wrong with me. I don't want to sit in a wheelchair. "It's just a precaution; just relax and I'll push you," the nurse calmly told me as she smiled. I already had to say out loud that I'm bleeding. And now I'm riding past everybody in a wheelchair. I felt like all the faces staring at me already knew what I didn't want to know or admit.

I nervously situated myself on the ultrasound table and waited, holding my breath, for the ultrasound tech to give an indication of anything. As expected, she didn't. She made small talk with me about the usual; weather outside, how many weeks along I was, what number pregnancy this was, how had I been feeling, etc. At one point during the ultrasound, she made a comment to another tech in the room, "Look; that's cute." In my mind, I imagined my baby's little heart beating away, or a hand near the face, or a tiny foot with little toes that were visible enough to make out on the screen. But she didn't say anything to me or elaborate any further on what she had been talking about. She sent me back to the chair of shame to wait for a nurse to push me into my actual room to wait for the results.

She pushed me down the hall, past the other patients who gazed at me as I walked past and felt their wandering minds trying to decide why I was there and what could be "wrong" with me. She put me in a room and shut the door. My heart started to sink, little by little. I didn't even want to know what the results were. As my mind raced through all the possible options, my body wanted to get up and leave, as panic again overtook me. Just go home. Leave. It doesn't matter what they say. Everything is going to be fine. No matter how much I worried, or how many times I went over all the possible scenarios in my head, nothing could have prepared my mommy heart for the ultimate reality of what was about to happen.

The "provider" came in and introduced herself. She then proceeded calmly, as if she was sharing with somebody what she had eaten for breakfast that morning, "So, there was no cardiac activity detected during the ultrasound. And you're 12 weeks pregnant according to our calculations, but the baby is only measuring 9 weeks. So it looks like the baby passed away about 3 weeks ago and your body is just now realizing it and trying to catch up – which is why you started bleeding today most likely. It should pass on its own no problem, now that the process has started, but if it doesn't we will remove it in 5 days. Do you have any questions?" Just like that, in one sweeping breath, she brought my whole world crashing down on top of me.

Do you remember that feeling from grade school, after falling from the monkey bars? Even though it's not that big of a deal to get the wind knocked out of you, which you don't find out until later, you're certain for a few seconds that you must be dying. Blurred vision, no breath, impossible to breathe, back hurts. That's what it felt like. I couldn't move. After she trailed off with "Do you have any questions?" I calmly answered "No," all the while in my mind I pictured myself screaming at her; "What the hell are you talking about??? What is wrong with you? Why would you say that?? How can you stand there and talk about this like it's nothing?" I left the emergency room numb, in complete disbelief about what had just happened, but to the best of my ability letting my new reality slowly sink in.

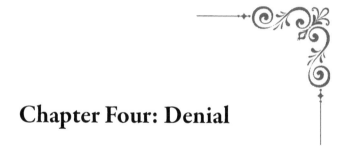

Chapter Four: Denial

I got home and began getting ready for bed, as by that time it was near-ly one o'clock in the morning. Everything about my life in that moment felt surreal. I wanted to pinch myself. Did that really just happen? All I've had is the most minor spotting. And I'm still pregnant. They saw a baby. Maybe everything is going to be fine and they made a mistake on the ultrasound. Maybe this will be one of those stories where I go back in a week for a regular checkup, have a follow up ultrasound, and there's a heartbeat. My mind settled on that notion for but a brief second, before I was reminded of the harsh and discomforting words that the practitioner had said right at the end of my appointment. My body should be able to take care of this on its own in a few days. "No. What my stupid body should know how to do is grow a baby. I've done it three times already. What is the problem this time?", I angrily retorted within myself.

For every moment that my heart had some glimpse of hope, my mind had a quick comeback to set me straight. Yes, there was a baby there. But it was measuring three weeks too small. Even though it's there still, it ob-viously isn't right. It can't be that far behind and be healthy, even if it is living. Yes, there was a baby there. But it had no heartbeat. The heart has to be beating for the body to be working and the baby to be alive. Yes, I've only had minor spotting, but that's because this is only the begin-ning of a process that is sure to come to completion. Either on its own, or with help from science and medical professionals. There's no coming back from this truth.

I fought and argued angrily within myself that entire night, as I tossed and turned. I barely slept. And in the morning, I got up and went to work. I put on my big girl panties, my game face, and I went. I wanted my day to be normal. I wanted to pretend nothing had happened. I was nowhere near coming to terms with what was going on and something within me had a drive to just keep functioning like I normally would, as though that would perhaps miraculously change something. I made it through the workday without it crossing my mind save for a couple of brief instances.

As I traveled home, I became so angry. It had been almost 24 hours since I'd started bleeding, and it was only for a little while... and then nothing. Now, I'd gone to work as though everything were normal, and literally not bled at all throughout the entire day. I felt completely normal, just as I had for the rest of the pregnancy, and nothing seemed different except for the lingering words from the previous night's appointment. "No cardiac activity."

I called my OBGYN's office, hoping for some sort of miracle when I talked to them. They know me. My history. They know I've had two successful pregnancies, and even carried over-sized twins past full term. Maybe when I spoke with them they would reassure me that sometimes this happens, but everything would be okay. They put me on a brief hold and then let me know I could come in after the weekend and see the doctor. "Anything else?" I quickly asked before the receptionist hung up. She seemed eager to get off the phone and just told me if anything changed or worsened over the weekend, to go back to the emergency room. Otherwise they would see me Monday and decide next steps. That wasn't the phone call I'd hoped for. And now I had to wait three days to hear a "real" doctor maybe tell me the same thing I already knew from my emergency room visit.

I decided, based on how well I felt and the fact that I needed to get my mind off what was (or wasn't, really, as nothing had changed) happening, that I'd take a trip to my parents' house. They lived only a couple of hours away at the beach, it was a nice drive, and I needed time to clear my head anyways. Maybe a change of scenery would somehow help me sort things out in my mind. If I was away from the daily routine in my usual comfort zone, with my still tarnished pregnancy, maybe it would sink in a bit.

I was fine for about an hour into the drive. Uneventful, not much to see, hardly any traffic, listening to the radio and cruising along. And then a wave of grief came over me. The funny thing about grief is it hits you when you least expect it. It could have been a song on the radio, a thought that had crossed through my mind, something somebody said, something I noticed.... it's not always easy to decipher the cause. It's impossible to predetermine when grief is going to encompass your thoughts and heart and cause a flood of emotion that can't be held back, no matter where you are.

I sobbed heavily for about 15 minutes before I was finally able to gain control over my emotions again. I didn't really know why, or what specifically I had been sobbing about. Miscarriage doesn't make sense. That's enough to make you crazy or cause a surge of emotions based solely on frustration and unknowns that are too much to try and process. The wealth of information, questions, and anxieties I had running through my mind at any given moment were sorely overwhelming.

My mind slowly began to grasp the sober realization that no matter what happened in the next few days or weeks, this pregnancy was not going to end the way I wanted it to; a healthy, happy baby. The reality slowly began to eat away at what once had been the dream of what life with this baby would be like. Little by little, as the reality became clearer, a little more of the dream of "what could have been" died along with my hopes.

Chapter Five: Looking for Answers

I had done some research after my doctor's appointment and discovered that there are several types of miscarriages; which I hadn't known previously. There is a "complete miscarriage," which is basically just what it sounds. Your body decides that this isn't going to work, for whatever reason, and expels the baby spontaneously. All of its own mind and accord. There is also an "incomplete miscarriage." This is when the body has started to expel tissue and membranes from the pregnancy (much like having a period) but there is still pregnancy related tissue in the uterus. A "missed miscarriage" is when the baby is dead, but the body has done nothing to expel the tissue, fetus, membranes, etc. and everything still remains as though the pregnancy were intact. There is also a threatened miscarriage. In this case, you may be bleeding or spotting but there is still a heartbeat and everything about the pregnancy appears normal. The trouble in this case is that spotting is often a normal part of pregnancy, but it could also mean that something has gone wrong and an impending miscarriage is likely (Moore, 2012).

In my opinion, the most frustrating part about most of miscarriage types is the waiting. As though pregnancy isn't stressful enough in a normal situation, you add one of these factors and it makes it a thousand times more unbearable. Now, you aren't just waiting for your first ultrasound, or to find out the sex of your baby, or to have your next appointment, or to go into labor – but you're waiting to find out if your baby is even going to survive or not and whether you're even going to be pregnant in a few weeks.

With my second pregnancy, the twins, I'd had a threatened miscarriage. It was terrifying. I started spotting at 14 weeks and went immediately to the emergency room. After an IV for hydration purposes (dehydration also can cause mirror symptoms to those experienced during a miscarriage), blood tests, urine sample, an ultrasound, lots of poking and prodding and examinations by several different people; the determination was made that everything about the pregnancy looked normal. After several hours in the emergency room, I was released to go home. My discharge paperwork said "threatened miscarriage." I will never forget reading how it was likely that my body may experience a miscarriage in the near future, but there was really no way to be sure, so just go home and prepare for that. Stay in bed, get lots of rest, drink lots of water and hope you don't start bleeding more – basically. Why is everybody so casual about everything when there is a life at stake here?

With this (my third) pregnancy, it was determined that I'd experienced an incomplete miscarriage, as the baby was already dead but there was obviously an entire baby and lots of other tissue and pregnancy related membranes remaining in the uterus. The options with an incomplete miscarriage are first waiting, and then acting. If the body does not expel *all* of the tissue on its own in a rather short period of time (5 days was recommended by my treating physician in the emergency room), then a medical procedure to remove everything from the uterus would have to be performed. This was not optional, unfortunately, as waiting longer than that put my body at high risk for infection or other serious problems, including too much blood loss.

The medical procedure that sometimes takes place in the case of a miscarriage is known as a dilation and curettage (D&C). It is basically a combination of what women know as a pap smear, with the added factors much like those that occur in an abortion. The cervix is opened/dilated with medical tools, if needed (sometimes it has opened on its own, especially if the miscarriage is in process already). Additional instruments are then used to scrape the entire lining of the uterus and remove everything that is left, in order to clear everything and get back to normal. In the case of an incomplete or missed miscarriage, it is not the same thing as an abortion simply because the fetus has already died. However, aside from that, there are many similarities.

I didn't want to know this. At all. This is too much information for me, I don't want to think about it ever having happened to anybody, and I certainly didn't want to think about the likelihood of it possibly happening to me. I had these occasional bouts of hope that my body would hurry up and figure out how to expel everything on its own. As much as I didn't want the process to continue, as for some reason while the baby was still there I felt there was some glimpse of hope (even though the reality said otherwise), just as much of me wanted to hurry up and get it over with.

Every now and then, the reminder would hit me again like a ton of bricks. My baby was dead. I was never going to see, hold, rock, comfort, or even touch my baby. As if it wasn't bad enough that my baby was dead; it was stuck inside me. I began to experience waves of contradictory emotions. Part of me wanted to go back to the emergency room and beg them to remove it right now. I don't want to wait for my body to figure this out; I want it out. I don't want a dead baby inside of me. It's broken. It's gone. However, just as quickly as I was able to process that emotion, a wave of grief and guilt would follow. I wanted my body to take as long as it possibly could when I realized that this was going to be the only time I ever had with my baby. That was it. Those last days were all that I'd ever know of my baby, who I'd never met but dearly loved and missed, and wanted with me for as long as possible.

I didn't really know what to think most of the time. I walked around feeling sort of like I was in a fog. There was so much weighing on my emotions, but it was impossible to process any one emotion fully and so I mostly just avoided it as much as possible and tried to carry out my daily routines as usual. Although I'd had reservations and concerns for several weeks in the pregnancy, I couldn't escape the cruel reality that my baby was in fact dead. The pregnancy began to feel like a plague that I just wanted to get rid of as quickly as possible. Part of me was guilty for feeling that way. My baby couldn't help that something had gone wrong, didn't deserve this, should stay with me as long as possible. But I more wanted to go back to normal, and be "clean" and move on to whatever would be the next step in the process.

In those last days I spent with my baby, before the miscarriage was complete, my mind toiled and grieved over so many things. What had once been a special, happy, amazing thing growing inside me was now dead. It was stuck there and I didn't want it to be. I wanted to be able to start over, and try again. Get a new baby there and do things differently so that I could ensure a better chance at success. Drink more water. Exercise more often. Zero caffeine. Less chocolate. Take more naps. Anything. I would do it. All of it. As my mind continued to detach from the bond that would have been, my body continued to process what had happened. As the process (physically and emotionally) continued, a new sense of "normalcy" set in, though it never stayed for long before waves of doubt and dread washed over me again.

Miscarriage is the loss of so much more than just a child. Everything I had known and looked forward to about the remainder of my pregnancy and how life would change in less than nine months, had suddenly come crashing down around me...never to be what I'd dreamed it would.

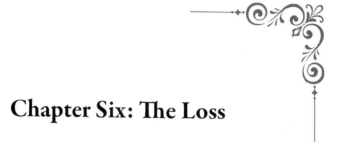

Chapter Six: The Loss

I will warn you in advance that this chapter is going to be graphic. Not because the details are necessary to understand the process, but because I wished throughout this entire experience that somebody would tell me what to expect. I had no idea if anything that was happening was normal. At moments I felt sure I was going to die, and wanted more than anything for someone to say "Oh, that very same thing happened to me when I had a miscarriage". Honestly. If you want or need to know the details, so you can understand the process and know what you can possibly expect, you're not alone. Your process of physically losing the baby or having a complete miscarriage may be different. However, the more people I ask, the more I hear that their experience was much like mine. I wish someone had told me.

I decided to head back home from my parents' house the following afternoon. I had been there just over 24 hours and the bleeding hadn't picked up much but was certainly more than the prior day, when it was almost non-existent. I was still feeling completely normal, all things considered, and was ready to just get back home and get busy or try and figure out what to do next.

About an hour into the drive, I started cramping. "This is weird...almost like right before getting my period," I thought. The cramps sort of came and went, but within about 30 minutes began to worsen. Shortly after that, I began to feel blood gushing every few minutes. I was in the middle of nowhere... no bathrooms or rest stops in sight, and obviously you can't just pull over and change your pad on the side of the road. To make matters worse, I now had two of my boys in the backseat (they had been visiting with grandparents and part of the reason for my trip was to pick them up and bring them home). They had no idea that anything had happened and were oblivious to the circumstance I was currently finding myself in.

As I grew in nervousness, anxiety, hesitation and uncertainty, I continued trying to appear as calm and normal as possible. I realized that the more still I sat and less I moved around, the less blood I was losing. I put the car on cruise control and did the best I could to keep my mind off things and sit rather still so as not to aggravate anything. The cramps worsened and soon I couldn't sit still enough to keep the blood from gushing out. I had to move around just to ease the discomfort and try to get in a position that was more bearable. In a matter of a few minutes, I knew the pad I was wearing had been soaked through already, and as I felt blood still gushing, I reached down to check my pant leg. To my surprise and bewilderment, still whilst trying to successfully drive the car, I realized my fingers were covered in blood. I grabbed an extra pad out of my purse and wiped my fingers on it; all the while getting more pissed off.

It was ridiculous. I felt like I was in the scene of a movie and had just been shot or something. I grabbed the window shade for my car and quickly slid it beneath my butt, hoping to protect my car upholstery. I was beginning to realize that the problem with an "incomplete miscarriage" is you never know if or when it's going to complete. It was not a pretty sight and I had certainly been unprepared for what was happening. Especially considering that not even an hour prior I'd been feeling completely normal and barely bleeding at all. Just like that, I was in the throes of a full on miscarriage, and it was horrible.

I made it home (another dreadfully unbearable and increasingly messy and uncomfortable 30 minutes) without much further incident, but I could feel the blood going further and further down my pant legs as it continued to slowly gush out every now and then. When I finally arrived in the driveway and stood up out of the car, I cannot even express accurately to you how much blood came gushing out. It immediately went all the way down both of my pant legs, and started dripping from the bottom. I left a little trail of blood spots from the car to the house, before rolling up my pant legs and getting as quickly as I could to the bathroom. I headed for the shower as there was obviously no alternative solution that would be successful. By that time, I was having cramps and pains that felt like labor.

I spent about an hour in the shower as the rest of the miscarriage took place. I thought back to my appointment a couple of days prior in the emergency room. The healthcare professional who I saw had told me, "Everything should pass on its own and a 9-week fetus is so small you may not even notice when it's lost." Well, unfortunately, I noticed. I passed several large (ping pong to golf ball sized) clots and eventually one that was bigger than a golf ball but smaller than a tennis ball. I could no longer hold it together mentally or emotionally, and began uncontrollably sobbing in the shower. I knew that was my baby.

I couldn't speak. I managed to scream for my husband, who came and helped me clean up what was in shower the best that he could, as I frantically tried to wash the rest of it down. There was blood everywhere and I absolutely wanted the large mass, which I knew was my baby, as far away from me as possible. My mind and body were completely repulsed by the image. All I could do was stare at it and scream. I had contractions and cramping for about fifteen more minutes; it so closely resembled labor that my spirit was completely devastated. This was so far from what I had envisioned, and from what childbirth is supposed to be like. No anticipation. No joy. No thankfulness. No life.

Further, that was *most certainly* not what I had envisioned when I pictured everything "passing on its own" and I "may not even notice," as my emergency room provider had so confidently stated. I had hoped maybe when I went to the bathroom at some point everything would pass. Or some here and some there. I didn't realize that I would labor and pass the entire thing all at once as though I were giving birth. Though not nearly as intense or painful, the process and physical experience was the same as dealing with labor and having a live baby. However, the emotional toll it took on me made it a thousand times worse than the pain of giving birth to a full-term baby.

Eventually the bleeding became steadier and lessened to the point I felt I could get out of the shower and get dressed again. I was completely paralyzed emotionally and I just wanted to crawl in bed and go to sleep, which is exactly what I did. I slept for several hours, right through dinner and my husband putting all of our other children to bed. At some point, I got up long enough to get some water, go to the bathroom, change the pad and get right back in bed for the night.

Chapter Seven: The Aftermath

The next day, early in the morning, I decided I would have to call in sick at work and take the day off. I had mild to moderate cramping, but felt absolutely exhausted. I had slept relatively well throughout the night, but didn't even have the energy to get out of bed and get anything to eat. Emotionally, I was completely drained and numb from the experience. Physically, I wondered mostly whether my body was suffering from such a great amount of blood loss so alarmingly quickly. I felt depressed at moments, completely void of hope or drive to achieve anything, but mainly still just completely numb. I was repulsed by my own body and that fact that I was stuck in the same room as a body that had completely failed me, and my baby. Nothing was right or how it was supposed to be and I could barely keep my composure mentally.

I stayed in bed almost that entire day following the miscarriage. It felt almost like I'd had the flu at times. The part when you don't feel nauseous anymore but your body is so drained that you need to replenish, but you're too tired to replenish because you're so drained. My husband brought me lots of water throughout the day and I finally had the energy to get up and get something to eat in the late afternoon. I felt somewhat better once I'd eaten, but a lingering fatigue still hung over me – both mentally and emotionally, as well as physically.

I'm the type who doesn't want to sit around at home and think about things. The sooner I can get my life back to normal and resume my usual activities, the sooner I can emotionally get over what happened and process the emotions more smoothly. The more normalcy, the better. I went to work the following day and resumed as though nothing had happened. Deep down inside, every time I talked to somebody, I felt like I should be telling them. "My baby died a few weeks ago, and yesterday finally left me forever." It seemed so anti-climactic to have lost a baby with no funeral, burial, official goodbye, recognition from friends and family, nothing...just lost. In the shower.

As often as I had the fleeting thought that maybe I should be telling people, it was quickly followed by the question and wonder of what would people think. I was only 12 weeks pregnant when I lost the baby, and we hadn't even been able to determine the sex yet. I felt like people would judge me and wonder how I could really be so greatly grieving something I didn't even really know. There was no name, no identity, but my baby was so much a part of me that was missing. My heart was so confused and my mind just toiled over the same questions throughout the days that followed. All the while, I put on my game face and lived through every day as though nothing had happened. I had to be strong for my husband, my kids, my job, myself. But not one part of me felt strong or able to endure what we were experiencing.

Over the next few days, I continued to bleed. I went to my follow up appointment with the midwife, which originally was to determine whether I would need a D&C or not. She asked me several questions about what had happened, being as lovingly sensitive as she possibly could and trying to reassure me that what I was going through was normal during a loss. She clarified the size of the clots/masses I had passed to ensure what she ultimately determined was the baby had in fact passed. She asked me if I wanted an ultrasound to make sure there were no remnants of the pregnancy left, which were cause for potential infection or other issues. I assured her that there was no way on earth that there was anything left in my uterus after what I had gone through a few days prior. Primarily, the thought of an ultrasound was more emotionally insulting than anything. At this stage, I should have been getting an ultrasound to check the baby's size and measurements and make sure things were progressing normally. Instead, I was being offered an ultrasound to determine if there were any pieces of the pregnancy that were left and needed to be forcefully removed. No, thank you. She gave me instructions for home: continue taking prenatal vitamins, get lots of rest, no intercourse for six weeks, no tampons, drink plenty of water, come back if bleeding gets worse or anything changes, wait at least three months to get pregnant (preferably one normal period). I cringed at the thought. Why on earth would I want to get pregnant again in the next three months and risk re-living this nightmare?

And so, we slowly and reluctantly started on the journey of "after miscarriage." It consumed our minds every single day. There wasn't a moment that went by that I didn't think or wonder about my baby. And if there was a moment when my mind wandered enough to forget for a second, I was whipped back to reality by the bleeding that continued to physically torment me day after day.

About seven or eight weeks post-miscarriage, I started obsessively scouring the internet trying to figure out what a "normal" amount of time bleeding would be. Although the bleeding had tapered off around six weeks, it had reinstated itself several days later as though we were starting all over again. I was already grossly irritated because the midwife had told me that my normal period should resume within 4-6 weeks. How the heck was my period going to go back to normal if I hadn't even stopped bleeding yet?

As I considered what she had said, coupled with the various things I was reading online, I realized what I've now come to know is the unfortunate reality about miscarriage. Not only do many people not talk about it, but those who do have varying levels of experience and recoveries. Further, the internet is a sea of conflicting information that does nothing more than leave you wondering. Or, alternatively, has you subscribed to somebody's one inconsequential blog post and mentally adhering to what is read within simply because there is one symptom that mirrors what you're going through and it feels good to be "normal" – even if only for a moment.

After several more days of bleeding, I decided I should go back to the doctor to get her feedback on what could potentially be going on. I started wondering if I should have had the dreaded and insulting ultrasound that had been offered to me at my last appointment. Regardless, at this point it was becoming obvious that something needed to change. I was ready to be done bleeding and get on with my life, without my body reminding me daily that something had gone wrong. Every time I bought another box of feminine pads I thought, "For sure, this is the last one." Yet it never was.

Chapter Eight: Lingering Emotional Turmoil

As you may have gathered by now, or maybe experienced yourself, the physical process of a miscarriage is ugly; both figuratively and in real time. It is tiresome and gruesome and seemingly unwarranted. Why should your body, which was trying so hard to create a beautiful little human being, have to endure such a continual mess of nonsense after already surviving the initial trauma that had occurred in the first place? That said, and greatly considering what's already known, the physical process of a miscarriage is pale in comparison to the emotional one. That of itself, given the description I've just shared of how my miscarriage progressed physically, should provide a pretty clear picture of just how unbearable the emotional process of a miscarriage is.

It's the little, unexpected occurrences that seem to create the most pain in the emotional aftermath of a miscarriage. The first one hit me like a ton of bricks not long after the miscarriage had begun. I had excitedly signed up for weekly reminder emails throughout the pregnancy; detailing what to expect, symptoms you could be experiencing, what changes might be happening, etc. as the pregnancy progressed. They came every Sunday. The week after the complete miscarriage had happened, I heard my phone ding – signifying an email had arrived – and absentmindedly picked it up and began reading. A wave of nausea and sudden grief came over me all at once as I read "You're thirteen weeks pregnant. This week will bring...".

I was appalled. The nerve of sending me this email. I quickly realized that to not get those emails for the remaining would have been twenty-seven weeks of my pregnancy, I needed to unsubscribe. As much as I wanted to not endure what I knew the next several moments would bring emotionally, I conjured up the nerve to do it because I knew the alternative was to feel this mini grief wave every week for the next twenty-seven weeks until this "would have been" pregnancy came to fruition on paper. I clicked the "unsubscribe" link at the bottom of the email which took me to my account on the website. I am subscribed to several different email threads through the website, for my other children and just parenthood in general. I found the one that signified this pregnancy and clicked the "stop getting these emails" link. Naturally, it led to a page that asked me what the reason for unsubscribing was. There, amidst the other usual suspects, was my reason. "This pregnancy ended in a miscarriage."

It hit me like a ton of bricks. It's one thing to endure it. It's quite another to see it in writing. To have to click the box that so blazingly shouts in six words what a lifetime of happiness could not fix. To subscribe to a "label" of someone who has had a miscarriage. To know what it feels like to be one of those. To feel the weight of what clicking that option means; in your heart, soul and body. Previously, I would have simply scanned over it and pretended it wasn't there. But now, I know. I know how it feels. I know the gritty details and gruesome experience it actually is. I know that something as miniscule as unsubscribing from an unwanted email becomes an emotionally charged experience; another thing to endure along the process of the miscarriage aftermath.

The next item on the agenda for enduring the aftermath would be the advertisements, flyers, mailers and free samples that started showing up at my house and on my computer screen. Naturally, the excitement of pregnancy brought on the desire to sign up and subscribe to as many things as possible. When shouting it from the rooftops doesn't seem enough, there are a flurry of places you can visit to "notify" you are pregnant and begin receiving constant invitations to sample, buy, try and add things to your baby inventory. Or, like us, if you aren't far enough along to announce your pregnancy yet, you can secretly enroll for a bunch of free things and it almost feels like everybody knows.

All the free stuff is great fun while you're pregnant, and fuels your excitement considerably. After a miscarriage, less fun. Far less fun. On numerous occasions, I considered an attempt at figuring out a way to get rid of all these "fun" advertisements that kept showing up in my mailbox, at my doorstep, or across the screen of a social media page. Ultimately, I determined that there would be no way to ever completely rid everything and there was always potential for something slipping through the cracks and showing up anyway. So, I just dealt with it instead. Things that came in the mail went straight to the recycle bin. Free samples went straight to the trash can or were stuck up high in the back of a kitchen cabinet where I could forget they existed. Advertisements about baby gear were ignored as best I could, or clicked with a placid request of "don't ever show me this again."

Finally, there are babies. Probably the most offensive of all the things that cause undue pain while in the process of recovering from a miscarriage. Babies everywhere. On a typical day, I think I can go for a while without seeing a baby. Maybe one here or there. After a miscarriage, the sea of babies seems endless. They're everywhere. Babies with moms, babies with dads, babies with grandmas, babies with hats, babies in strollers, sleeping babies, babies laughing in the distance, babies in car seats, babies in car windows, babies crying, and worst of all – babies looking at me. An unknowing mother, holding her baby, standing in front of me in line at a checkout lane; her baby suddenly turns and makes eye contact, smiling away. My face smiles back, while my heart cries out in pain. A silent tear falls, rolling down my cheek and under my chin, dropping off my face and landing on my hand. A small, warm droplet that signifies such great pain. A heart silently suffering. A small life, never known, save for within the body of the mother whose heart now aches.

Chapter Nine: The Ugly War Within

An unfortunate reality of our human nature is always wanting to have an explanation for the "why" in life. No matter how hard we try to ignore it, forget about it, pretend it doesn't exist, or just deal with it as best we can and move past, it's always there. I have noticed especially when it comes to something painful or tragic, the why question is the one that is consistently staring us right in the face. As if what's going on is not already bad enough, add the problem of the wandering mind trying to figure out the why of everything, and you've got yourself a real-life internal nightmare.

Unfortunately, when it comes to miscarriage, trying to figure out the "why" entails trying to nail down a reason for what went wrong. In some cases when it comes to miscarriage, the reason is more easily identifiable. There would likely be some testing involved to rule out whether it was sperm, egg, uterus, or some other problem before an ultimate determination was made. I've learned from experience with friends and acquaintances that this is the case specifically if there has been more than one miscarriage. However, in the majority of cases (namely because miscarriage is actually fairly common), the culprit isn't known and that is widely acceptable within the medical field. The problem with this is when you're the person who had the miscarriage, rather than the medical field, not knowing simply doesn't suffice.

As the weeks went on, I began to become increasingly frustrated. I knew, obviously (having had two prior successful pregnancies without incident), it wasn't an issue with either myself or my husband. Even though I knew that in my head, I couldn't settle myself without the why question answered. I began to go over and over everything in my mind; a constant cycle of thoughts and unanswered questions that drove me crazy but I couldn't get away from. The harder I tried to just accept the fact that we would never know the reason for our miscarriage, the more frustrating it became that we didn't know the reason.

Naturally, when a situation is negatively affecting a person, it inadvertently can begin to take an emotional toll on the relationships they are in as well. Though we tried to avoid this as much as we possibly could, we definitely had a rough patch. There were plenty of things that shouldn't have been said, that were said. As we both searched the internet for possible answers to the "why" question that remained looming over us, the results included a variety of options for potential miscarriage causes that included both the male and female in possibilities. The continual search for answers and frustration of not knowing what the answer was, led to some difficult encounters between us. We blamed ourselves. We blamed each other. We said hurtful things. We cried and mourned together. We shouted and questioned our part, placed blame on one another and generally toiled over what it could have been that caused us to get to where we were now. It was ugly. It was bumpy. We each processed in our own way, but most importantly at some point we resolved that no matter what, we were going to make it. This miscarriage had happened to both of us, and we were the only two in that moment who could feel what it felt like to be in our shoes, and we needed each other.

As though the emotional struggle wasn't enough, I continued to bleed for weeks on end after the miscarriage had completed. The six weeks when my period was supposedly going to potentially resume, came and went. I was still bleeding away just as I had been since the miscarriage had happened. There was nothing that happened to signify any change or progression of healing, just consistent bleeding. Finally, about eight weeks after the miscarriage, I made an appointment to go back in and get checked. I was starting to regret not having had the ultrasound that would have added insult to injury at the time when the miscarriage had just happened. Now, I had a constant reminder of the miscarriage every day and it had been over two months.

She didn't have much for suggestion at the appointment, besides knowing for sure that everything was okay physically as far as infection, or any other potential problems, based on test results at the appointment. Her best guess was that my body simply was on an endless loop of hormonal cycling and probably need a bit of a shock to get it restarted and hopefully back to normal. There were several options for this, one of which was birth control pills. I knew for a fact that we wanted to try and get pregnant again soon, and thus opted to not go back on the birth control pills just to come off them again; although the doctor was sure this would work to get my body regulated.

I opted for the second recommendation she had, which she was less certain would work, but was willing to try. Apparently, (why had I never heard this before??) the prostaglandin (hormone/menstrual) cycle can be lessened or even stopped simply by taking a round of Ibuprofen. She put me on prescription Ibuprofen three times a day (every 8 hours around the clock) for seven days. She told me not to miss any doses, and to continue for the entire seven days even if the bleeding seemed to lessen at any point. As I gathered my things and readied to leave, she remarked "Come back if you need anything. Maybe I'll see you this Fall when you're pregnant again!" I know she didn't mean anything by that comment, but this takes us reeling backwards to the prior chapter of lingering emotional turmoil. Ouch. Nothing like putting the pressure on.

I left; mostly thankful I hadn't needed an ultrasound. The idea of having an ultrasound of an empty uterus when I knew exactly how many weeks pregnant I should have been seemed insulting far beyond anything else I could have endured at that point. I wanted to completely forget I even had a uterus, much less check to see whether it was for sure completely empty or not like it was supposed to be at this point. Thinking about my empty uterus, of course, set me back on the cycle of trying to answer "Why?". Much to my surprise, within a few days of starting the Ibuprofen regimen, bleeding lessened and almost completely stopped. By the time the seven days was over, it had stopped enough for me to consider myself not bleeding anymore.

Unfortunately, not bleeding lasted about five to seven days before it started up again. I was so tired, at that point, of even thinking about it anymore, I just resolved myself to the fact that I was going to be bleeding for possibly the rest of my life, and gave up. As frustrating as it was, the more I internet searched and tried to figure out what was "normal" for bleeding after miscarriage, the less answers I really had. There is little information out there regarding miscarriage, and the information that IS out there seemed to completely miss the topics I needed answers to, or was so convoluted because of varying degrees of information, it simply wasn't helpful.

Thankfully, in about another week, the bleeding stopped completely. I had bled for twelve weeks total post-miscarriage. Honestly, I consider all of it the miscarriage. The miscarriage didn't end the day I lost the baby, because for the three months afterward my body wasn't doing what it was obviously normally supposed to. Nor was it doing anything it would have been had I still been pregnant as expected. It was weird, frustrating, abnormal, exhausting, infuriating, tiresome, and quite frankly expensive (I seriously must have used about three thousand pads). And though the physical aspect of the miscarriage finally ended after twelve weeks, the emotional, it seemed, could continue forever.

Chapter Ten: Good Intentions

As with so many other things in life, when people encounter a difficult situation, others often don't know what to say. Although the common thread among us is that we each know there isn't anything that could be said that would change the situation, people always still search for something to say. Unfortunately, if people don't feel like they can figure out the exact thing to say, they end up not saying anything at all. The flip side of that coin, is the people who say whatever comes to mind or feel like they have all the advice in the world to offer that would be helpful.

There are people who will avoid the topic of your miscarriage like the plague and don't want to bring it up or discuss it, seem awkward when you encounter them because they seemingly don't have a thing to say, or simply change the subject as soon as it's brought up. Those people will make you feel like your baby didn't matter. It will seem like they couldn't possibly care about you because if they do, how could they possibly avoid it and act like nothing is wrong when you're heartbroken and feel like you're crumbling inside. The truth is, they simply don't know how to react. Pain makes people uncomfortable; seeing someone we care about in pain is even more upsetting and generally brings a lack of confidence and uncertainty in even the closest of relationships.

The best way you could respond in this case is, most importantly, is don't let it get to you. Understand that people are not ill intentioned, they simply don't know what to do. Be honest and keep the lines of communication open. Tell people that you are hurting. Let them know that you don't want to talk about your miscarriage but it helps if they ask how you're doing. Everybody processes grief differently, but if you know something that helps you (meals, gifts, time spent together, trips, talking about things, getting your mind off things, walking, etc.) – tell people. Acknowledge that you don't need them to say anything specific, and you aren't expecting them to say anything that is going to fix what happened, but it helps if you don't avoid it like it is the elephant in the room and pretend it isn't there.

There are others who will give you every possible bit of advice they can possibly think of, in hopes of lessening what you're going through somehow. As though you haven't already explored every option and thought of every solution, and tried every remedy, they feel there's some piece of advice to offer that would be especially meaningful to you somehow. During the course of recovery, I heard everything from pregnancy advice (including how soon to get pregnant, why I should wait to get pregnant, why I should get pregnant again immediately, why I was less likely to have a miscarriage this time if I got pregnant again...) to fertility information. For example, did you know you're more fertile immediately after having a miscarriage and that is supposedly the best time to try getting pregnant again? Now why on earth would I completely disregard the advice of my healthcare practitioner, because you (a well-meaning acquaintance) decided to tell me what you read online about when I should get pregnant?

What I learned as I got tidbits of random advice from various people, is that they simply have the same problem as the first group who wants to avoid the discussion of miscarriage at all costs. They don't know what to say. I think oftentimes they search to find out more about miscarriage, simply because it's not often discussed as we know, and end up with some piece of information they must think is important. Obviously, if they're bringing it up, it is well intentioned. Unfortunately, it usually isn't very helpful. I found it easiest in these cases to just smile and say, "thank you."

There's no point in getting frustrated, there's no need to share your personal business (such as the timeline for when you plan to get pregnant again), there's no need to entertain a conversation regarding their advice or what you intend to do with it. And again, don't take it personally.

There's one piece of advice that stood out above all others. I'm not sure whether it's because I heard it more than any other advice, or because it's the advice I wish I could have taken, but didn't. Numerous people told me, from shortly after it first happened, that it would help if we named the baby. At first, I brushed it off as a crazy idea; how could I name a baby when I didn't even know if it was a boy or a girl? There's more advice for that question as well. Choose a unisex name that would work for whether the baby had been a boy or a girl. At some point, I seriously considered it. I brought it up to my husband in a passing conversation, "Someone told me we should name the baby... at least then when we talked about it, it wouldn't be so awkward because we could call it something." But, at no point did it become something that felt right or comfortable for us to do.

This may be advice you have heard, and if not is most likely something you will hear at some point. I have friends who have had miscarriages who have named the baby. I absolutely think it is something you should do if you feel like it would help you. For me, even the thought of naming the baby brought so much trepidation. I even attempted mentally at some point to come up with a name that would work or feel "acceptable." But the more I tried to name the baby, the more I felt ill at ease with the idea. It felt forced. Like something that needed to happen just so that the baby could have a name for convenience sake when it came to discussion or memorializing. Naming the baby wouldn't change the fact that I didn't know whether it was a boy or a girl, and neither would it change anything else.

As much as I wanted to name the baby, the more I thought about it the more it simply frustrated me that I didn't know if it was a boy or a girl. What I wouldn't give to go backwards and have begged them to try and figure it out before I had the miscarriage, so we could have known. But we don't. We never will. I felt like I would be dishonoring my baby in some way by giving a "unisex" name, because that baby is precious to me. Names are a big deal for us. All our children's names have been chosen with much thought, prayer, consideration, and are posted proudly on plaques in our home. Their names are chosen for who they are, and who they've become is more special because of the names we have chosen for them. I can't give that same gift to the baby I'll never meet because the meaning wouldn't be the same; even though I love that little person endlessly. As much as it broke my heart to not name the baby, I couldn't bring myself to do it. My baby is no less important because there is no name; my angel sings among the others, in Heaven with our Jesus.

So, we didn't name our baby. And we didn't try to get pregnant on anyone else's recommended time schedule of efficiency. I didn't try the weird herbs or over the counter remedies for bleeding, or fertility. I made it a point to not avoid the people who seemed terrified of what they would need to say; instead I approached them and generated conversation myself, finding that they were much more engageable once the ice was broken. I didn't share more information than I felt I needed to, but certainly didn't hesitate to share when it felt right to get something off my chest.

Do the best you can to wade through the sea of good intentions. I often think about how I approached people who'd had a miscarriage before I had experienced it myself. I remember that I was the person who didn't know what to say, or had random advice, or had the same questions they did and felt it necessary to ask for some reason – as though they may have some mystical answer they could pull from the atmosphere to appease my curiosity. I was that person and I in no way was ill intentioned, I simply didn't know any better. When I keep myself in that mindset, it gives me the ability to have a lot more grace to those who are "that person" in my life now. If they're naïve enough to be that person, in some way,

I'm thankful. I pray they never experience miscarriage personally and can keep that naivete that comes with not knowing what it's like.

Chapter Eleven: Now What?

A tiny sadness hung over me most days as I attempted to move on and continue living life as though things were normal. Going from being pregnant and planning what life will be like in the upcoming months, to being not pregnant again and knowing that the upcoming months will bring nothing but reminders of what should have been, is quite an adjustment. My baby's due date was December 16th; we were so excited to have a Christmas baby to introduce to everybody at an already special time of celebration for our families. The pregnancy announcements we had sent out one week and three days before our baby had passed away alluded to the greatest Christmas gift of all, who would be joining our family just in time for the holiday.

Nothing was normal. Every Friday, I added another week in my mind. "I would be 14 weeks today. I would have been 20 weeks today." I felt like I was living someone else's life. I knew my real life was out there somewhere and my mind wanted to figure out a way to get back to it. This life I was in seemed empty. I was going through the motions, but it felt like someone else's. I didn't really know what I was supposed to do with it. I'd gone from anticipation to devastation, in an instant. In the middle of a grocery store with a cart filled to overflowing. I took my prenatal vitamins every day like I had been before the miscarriage. But, no matter what I did, nothing seemed to make sense. Everything seemed inherently meaningless.

I dreamed often of my baby. I knew my baby was in Heaven; safe, loved, warm, well cared for, happy. In some ways I was jealous. How amazing would it be to never have experienced any of the pain that life on this earth brings, but to wake up for the first time and be in the presence of Jesus. This brought my heart some small comfort. I could see my baby in my dreams, though I never saw the face; but I knew my baby was okay. I often woke up with tears streaming down my cheeks and onto my pillow. I know I will be reunited with my baby one day; although my spirit hurts now, one day we will rejoice together. I fully intended for this stage of grieving I was in to last at least until my baby's due date. But just as suddenly as we'd found ourselves plopped in the middle of this unwanted nightmare, another surprise came our way.

I never had a period after my seemingly eternal miscarriage had finally ended and I stopped bleeding after twelve weeks. I didn't think about it much at first, counting my blessings and figuring my body had bled enough to last a lifetime and could take a few months off having a period and I wouldn't mind a bit. But then, after about six or seven weeks, I started wondering what exactly could be going on. It was in reverse this time. Go backwards and do it all again, but the other direction. I had wanted nothing more for three months than to stop bleeding, and here I was wondering when my period was going to come so I could be normal again and move on to whatever the next step would be.

When nothing changed still, after a few more days, I finally decided to take a pregnancy test. In many ways I felt like the twelve-week loss had allowed me plenty of time to grieve and process what had happened. We had settled into a new routine of normalcy; not being pregnant and not thinking "baby" all the time. Just spending time with our other kids, being together, thanking God for our blessings and doing the best we could to keep joy and hope alive in our souls. But, at the thought of taking a pregnancy test, a wave of nausea accompanied by endless wandering worries began to fill my mind. Uncertainty consumed my thoughts once again, but for different reasons this time.

Suddenly, I didn't know what to think or how to process this moment all over again. I was about to take a pregnancy test. This moment should be exciting. Yet, as surely as this very same moment several months ago brought excitement, all of the baggage that was now associated with that memory meant something completely different. "What if I am pregnant? Do I really want to be pregnant again and risk doing this all over? What if I'm not pregnant? Why don't I have my period? Did the miscarriage cause some kind of damage and now I'll never be able to get pregnant again? Am I already pregnant again? What if I am and it's another miscarriage? How will I know if there is something I should do differently?" I hushed all the questions that were racing through my mind, and decided to just hurry up and get it over with.

I didn't have to wait long for the second pink "pregnant" line to show up. It was dark. Really dark. Two lines. Pregnant. I just sat there for a moment; blankly staring at the positive test result. My next inclination was to grab my phone and search the internet for "What does it mean when the second line is so dark?" All the pregnancy tests I'd taken in the past, I'd never seen a line that dark. Apparently, the darker the line, the greater the influx of hormones – meaning you are most likely farther along the darker the line is. Well, that line was dark.

I sat down on the floor and leaned against the bathroom wall; taking a few big, deep breaths as I did so. I wanted to be excited. I wanted to be as excited for this baby as I was the last one. But the hurt... it was there. In my mind, my heart, my soul, my body. I ached. I wanted that baby. The baby that was gone. I wanted to know that baby. I didn't want a replacement baby to make me feel better about the baby I'd lost. As quickly as those feelings overtook me, I was met with even stronger feelings of guilt over not being as excited about this baby because of the loss of the last one.

I resolved in that moment that I would not let fear be the driving force behind this pregnancy because of what had happened. I survived a miscarriage once, and if I had another one, I would survive that one too.

At least in the future if I experienced another miscarriage, I would know what to expect. Not knowing what was coming or what my body was going to endure felt like half the difficulty with the miscarriage. I knew that fear and stress aren't healthy for a pregnancy, and I made it my mission to hope, feel, joy, cherish, anticipate and do all the normal things I normally would have done during pregnancy, before I'd experienced miscarriage.

And just like that, a new pregnancy adventure had begun.

Epilogue

Our rainbow boy came one year and eleven days after my miscarriage. As beautiful as he is, and thankful as I am, it doesn't change anything about the miscarriage. It's not any easier to miss that baby, or wonder about that baby, or remember what I endured emotionally or physically. But it reminds me that God is faithful. He loves us. He wants good for us. He wants to bless us. He has a plan up His sleeve. I'm thankful that my heart knows miscarriage, so I can love on and cry with those whose hearts are now experiencing it. I am humbled by the minute understanding I have of what loss feels like, and my heart is forever changed in relating to those who endure numerous losses, or failed IVF cycles, or simply can't get pregnant.

I'll never know what my baby looked like. I'll never even know if it was a boy or a girl. I couldn't name my baby for that reason, and so now it will forever linger as "the baby" who was lost. A piece of us that is gone forever. It's hard to explain what it feels like to be madly in love with someone you've never met, and you know you'll never get to meet. I fell in love with a stranger; loved a child I'll never meet. And my heart grieves because I love and miss that stranger, who left me before I could even give one kiss or caress in motherly love. I will never touch the baby soft skin, or see what we had in common, or know what color the eyes were, or cuddle under the blankets on a cold winter morning. But nonetheless, I love. I ache. I feel. I miss. I grieve.

The FACT is that miscarriage hurts. There's nothing I could have done to prevent it, or change it, or make it better. It wasn't my fault.

It was just one of those things that happens. We will never know the "why". But even if we did, it still wouldn't change anything. It happened. It hurt. Not just emotionally, but physically as well. It took a long time to process. I felt trapped inside my own body, and I wanted to get out. I needed some alone time to be separated from me, but there I was every day when I looked in the mirror.

It's hard to understand and even harder to explain. I'm so in love with that baby. I will forever miss that baby. A little piece of my heart died with that baby. Yet, I never even met that baby. Nobody can understand what it's like to be in love with a stranger, unless they've been through it themselves. Here's what I know for sure. You'll need help. TALK about it. Share about it. Write about it. Cry about it. Scream about it. You need friends, family, strangers, church, support groups, grief counseling. You need some of it; you may need all of it. Together we are stronger. It's okay to cry and it's definitely okay to let others cry with you. Ignore the people who say the things that seem senseless or insensitive. They simply don't know what to say, and they're doing the best they can.

Ask questions. Even the ones that seem like nobody would want to be asked. Ask about the process. Ask if what your body is doing is normal. Don't be embarrassed. Reach out to others who have had a miscarriage. And most of all, hang in there. Love yourself and your body for how hard it tried. Lean on your faith. If you've lost faith, find someone who still has it... or who can look back on a miscarriage with faith intact and know why it's okay, even if it doesn't make sense. It's hard, but you'll make it.

Miscarriage is ugly, but it's real. It will be easier than it is right now, if you're going through a miscarriage. It gets better than it feels right now. Keep the faith, keep the hope; stay surrounded by people who love and care for you. Do whatever helps you grieve. Find ways to remember your baby that are meaningful to you and your partner. You'll make it out alive and stronger on the other side. Promise.

Psalm 34:18
The Lord is close to the brokenhearted;
he rescues those whose spirits are crushed.

References

Moore, K. (2012, July 11). *What is a Miscarriage?* Retrieved from Health Line: http://www.healthline.com/health/miscarriage#Overview1

About the Author

Vanessa lives in central California with her husband and four children. She has her Master's Degree in Early Childhood Education and has worked as a professor for a local community college for three years. In her spare time she enjoys baking, reading, spending time outdoors with her family and movie nights with her husband.

Made in the USA
Monee, IL
01 June 2021

70005315R00028